The collected works of

Stuart McWilliam

Aka

The Red Rose Man

In loving memory of his dear wife Marion

To Jan.

Enjoy the Poems

Stuart.

Marion

Thank you for our married bliss

I still remember our very first kiss

I remember the where and the how

And the place was Quarry Knowe

Between Bellsmyre and Castlehill

There is fixed a great divide

But I am happy you crossed it

And so became my bride.

We still hold hands as we walk along

As in our hearts we share dance and song

For it is together we belong.

For fifty years we have shared this life

Thank you for being my wife,

I thank you for your love and care

When times were tough, you were always
there.

Fifty years is a long, long way

And I love you more each passing day.

That is all I can say 'the Noo' ,

And thank you for being just you.

Thank you Marion

Love Stuart

Ode to the Mill

Standing here in Castle Street

Where history and modernity meet

On my left I watch in awe

As a mechanical dinosaur munches

And on red bricks does gnaw

This old mill ground barley and maize

Producing flour in halcyon days

Cooked and boiled by steam

Part of the process of the Whisky dream

A place of legend and folklore

Tales from workers gone before

Sadly now a derelict eyesore

Whisky distilling, no more

Stories abound, too many to tell

Do you remember that pungent smell?

Bottling whisky still remains

No longer the milling of grains

Across the road new beginnings

Construction of new Council buildings

Will this lead to town regeneration

Can you feel a good vibration?

Will our town like the phoenix rise?

Will we experience a big surprise?

Will Dumbarton climb up the ranks?

Free from austerity and food banks.

Just Champion

(Printed Lennox Herald)

Levengrove Park a resplendent scene

A setting fitting for a queen

The pipes were skirling, kilts were swirling

The drums were beating

Grand pipe bands, a stirring meeting

The Park adorned in splendour

As pipes and drums, reels marches laments
did render

A sight so bright it did us hearten

With the colourful display of tartan

A new discovery today I made

Amidst all the tartan plaid

I knew that pipes had chanter and drones

But did you know that Sporrans

Were designed to carry mobile phones!

The mace throwers were so thrilling

As in to the air they sent them birling

And round their backs were twirling

Catching them with either hand, how grand

What about the Grand Finale

The massed pipe bands in full array

The ending to a perfect day

Tinged with sadness at the end

As on my way home I did wend

The memory of my late dear wife

And my very best friend

Still I'm grateful for a wonderful life.

Early Morning Story

Beneath the canopy of dark lowering cloud

Bright shining light of early morn

Silver blue streaked with wisps of white

Another day is born

Trees adorned in autumnal glory

Another chapter in life's story

Leaves of amber and of gold

Nature's beauty does unfold

Man with limited power and might

Could not create such a sight

Look around this earthly realm

Surely God is at the helm

The seasons come and go

Times to plant, times to sow

Times to nurture, times to grow

Times to harvest, times to mow

Our earthly sojourn is bound by time

Sometimes in life mountains to climb

Then find peaceful valleys to recline

Enjoy the wonders of God's design

Seasons of our lives, anticipation of spring

The warmth of sunshine summer does bring

In autumn the slowing down, leaves turning brown

Winters cold, and snow comes down

River of Love

The river of love flows gently through life

When you meet the beautiful woman

You marry, she becomes your wife

Sharing good times as well as troubles and strife.

Romance bubbling up like the rivers source

Sweeping forwards as it follows its course

Speeding through rapids, slowing round bends

Ebbing and flowing, knowing no ends

Thundering through rocks, cascading over falls

Contained by the banks, caressing enthralls

Lapping against the sandy shore

Flowing on strongly – for evermore

Finally discharging in to the sea

Coming together like you and me

Becoming part of the great Ocean

Like us embraced in lasting devotion

Softly and Sweetly

Softly and sweetly, you enter my mind

My darling you were so gentle and kind

Now feeling your presence I find

Memories of my Lady, so genteel and refined

In the evening as the shadows fall

Sweet thoughts of you I recall

Remembering you, my lovely Dresden doll

You were my life, you were my all

Now as my memories drift

Thoughts of you give me a lift

You raised me up to a higher plain

I'm longing to see and hold you again

Public Inconveniences

It is not by Royal Decree

To close public toilets by Royal Wee

It is penny pinching governments

Why not rent them out to Loo-Tenants

Once upon a time

We could spend a penny

Bringing great relief to many

Now we face trouble and distress

We are no longer flushed with success

Closing down well-kept loos

Diligently cleaned by attendant crews

Spotlessly clean, deodorized

Toilets for the civilized

New toilets are automated

Not recommended nor highly rated

Not for the loos of bowel

Nor the constipated

Don't hold your breath

Or anything else for that matter

Just cross your legs

And hold your watter.

Protestors Without a Cause

Protestors without a cause

Protestors in Trafalgar Square

Anti-American, sowing despair

Very, very, very unfair

In this same square, nineteen forty-five

Celebrations for the end of war

Thank you America – What for?

Today we are free, we are alive

What has Europe done for us?

The conflict, carnage of two world wars

This is a minus, not a plus

Protestors why are you making such a fuss

With the USA aid

There would have been a victory parade

Listen carefully protesting man and woman

Now you would be speaking German

Robbed of liberty, without choice

You would not have a protesting voice

Remember those who died for liberty

Setting you and I free

Distant Thoughts

Describe to me will you please

Speak to me words that ease

Sunset on a lonely beach

Ache in my heart, you are out of reach

Absence makes the heart grow fonder

It is hard when you are over yonder

Far beyond my arms embrace

Still I picture your lovely face

From a distance too far to travel

Thoughts of you, my mind unravel

Close to you I long to be

Please my darling, return to me

In the tenderness of my heart

I wish that we were not apart

Loneliness is a forsaken place

I long to see you, face to face

Now and Then

September nineteen thirty-nine

Declaration of war, a worrying time

A generation revisiting the same scene

Europe enmeshed in the war of 1914-18

Britain was then made of stern stuff

They stood up and cried "Enough"!

We have seen this all before

The slaughter and carnage of war

The people then, courageous and brave

Determined to fight, their freedom to save

With every fibre of their being did render

Fight to the death – No Surrender

That was then, what about now?

What a lonely furrow do we plough?

A united Europe, freedom to trade

Certainly not this political union charade

Germany, before with military might

Could not defeat us, or rob us of our right

Now they use a different policy

To bring us down economically

Britain now once more must make a stand

Restore the freedom to our land

Once again, just as before

Let us hear the Lion's roar

Open up the world trading door

No more talk of doom and gloom

Let's get back to Boom and Boom

October Evening

(Printed Lennox Herald)

Light is fading as I stroll

Over old Dumbarton Bridge

Under the archway may lurk a troll

Street lamps light up the trees

Bedecked with autumn coloured leaves

It is a truly magical sight

On this Halloween night

The River Leven ebb tide gathers pace

Turbulent waters into the Clyde race

Beneath the widespread branches of the trees

On the ground a carpet of fallen leaves

The evening air is silently still

Bringing a feeling of ghostly chill

Night has come, the daylight ended

Darkness on the scene descended

Childhood memories flood my mind

Déjà vu revisiting times behind

Nature is a wondrous thing

Lifting spirits and hearts to sing

The joy of living, people we met

Good times shared – No regret

Embrace the scenes all around

Like you are standing on holy ground

Escape from the pressure and strife

Enjoy to the full each day of life

Wedding of the Month

Wedding of the month, Earldom of Dumbarton

In the merry month of May

Daniel and Alice had their wedding day

Ceremony held at the church of St Pat's

Ladies adorned with their beautiful hats

After the blessings and the mass

Off to the reception in the house of glass

The venue at Loch Lomond shore

Fantastic setting, service great – could not ask
for more

Daniel a guy so cool

Keen supporter of Liverpool

Alice, I believe loves to shop

Daniel prefers to visit The Kop

Alice, beautiful, dressed like a queen

Accompanied by a bevy of maids so serene

A day to remember all of your life

Sun shone when you became man and wife

May your journey together be full of love

Filled with God's blessings from above

Living and loving day by day

Inspired by the memory of your wedding in May

Loneliness

Loneliness is not a happy place

God did not intend it for the human race

Some may describe it Kismet – Fate

God decided Man must have a mate

Friends and family can us surround

But we can still live in lonely ground

Being shy, retiring, often afraid

Fear of felling not making the grade

Then one day as if by chance

A relationship becomes a romance

From emptiness and low self esteem

You're now a king, you have met your Queen

You are now seated on a throne

Fulfilled and loved, no longer alone

Now uplifted raised high above

Totally enchanted by her love

Your lives together are full of joy

Children arrive, a girl and a boy

It feels just so right

Filled with happiness and delight

Then that day, that day of dread

My darling you are gone, you are dead

Now once again I'm all alone

A place I do not want to be

Oh how I miss your warm embrace

Your lovely smile, your sweetest kiss

Now in my heart I ache with pain

Until we are together again

Love

Love is when two lives combined

As two become one intertwined

Drawn together sharing devotion

Love is such a strong emotion

In marriage, vows we make

It's all about give and take

Learning to be caring and sharing

To achieve a perfect pairing

Your wife, your husband, start to end

Your confidante, your best friend

When days may be dark and drear

Always there to smile and cheer

So through all the passing years
Sharing hopes, dreams and fears
Sharing still when we first begun
As a pair we are truly one

Marion, my magnificent wife
How you filled our married life
You were the first lady of fashion and style
And, Oh! that entrancing smile

Marion, my life with you has been a dream
My beautiful wife with eyes of green
The most gorgeous girl I've ever seen
I shall never ever forget
That wonderful night we met

Silence

When silence speaks

It is profound

When sweetness our minds surround

No words spoken, not a sound

We enter in to hold ground

In the silence of sweet communion

The souls of Saints and God in union

As weary souls this journey trod

Stop to hear the still voice of God

For men and women of every age

Thank our god for words and language

For if our God had no words iterated

The world would not have been created

So thank we all for our God of Glory

Now that we have heard this wondrous story

How before this world begun

God promised salvation through His Son

God it was your eternal plan

To bring redemption to sinner Man

It was to sinners Jesus came

To glorify his Father's name

Cleansing us from guilt and shame

So thank we all our God

Who spared the sinner from the chastening rod

To change and make us realise

We have an eternal home in Paradise

Smile of My Life

Can I compare you to a summer day

Your beautiful smile, a sunbeam ray

Missed you when you were away

Don't go my love – please stay

Fill my life with love and care

When we are apart it's hard to bear

My happiness is complete when you are near

Being close to you, I want you here

Like a song of love to me you cling

Our voices blend when we sing

When we are together and we dance

We share our love, our true romance

With you I reached the pinnacle of life

When we married, you became my wife

Throughout our live I did you adore

I could not have asked for more

My darling, I loved you right from the start

Even more now we are finally apart

My memories forever filled by you

My lovely lady – who smiled from her heart

Hello

Hello, How are you today?

Has happiness come your way?

Has the sky been brightest blue?

Or are you toiling under clouds of grey

Life is fragile like a silver thread

Do you find a reason to get up out of bed

Are you a person with love to share

To bring love and happiness, show you care

Loneliness is a place of isolation

Feeling lost, no consolation

Knowing only disappointment and dismay

Longing for love and affection to come your
way

You have been reticent and shy

Love seems to have passed you by

Relationships have come and gone

Leaving you now all alone

Then one day – out of the blue

You love someone, who loves you

This meeting quite by chance

Blossomed into a life long romance

What about the children

Children of this world are alarmed

As by us adults you are being murdered,
mutilated and harmed

Instead of love, care and nurture

You are being robbed of your rightful future

Voices of children cry out in despair

Abandoned by adults who do not care.

Into this wonderful world you were born

Yet you suffer malice abuse and scorn

Adults who have power and rule

Why are you so angry and cruel

Act now before it is too late

Leant to love and be compassionate

Adults of the human race

Make this world for children a happy place

Teach them in this life to cope

Fill them with love, joy and hope

Adults do not be guilty of neglect

Treat your children with respect

That they may grow up honest and true

To follow a good example set by you

Olympic Reflections

Strong competition, wonderful feats

Unfortunately still some cheats

Athletes going through their paces

Jumping, diving, lifting, cycling, running races

Contestants of every colour race and creed

Leaders of the nations follow their lead

Overcome your differences put an end to greed

Turn your weapons in to tractors, feed those in
need

So many pictures of the winners joy

But what about the picture of that little Syrian
boy?

Suffering from a bomb blast from mans
inhumanity

As they carry out acts of depravity

O how our hearts long an yearn

When will we ever learn

When will this mindless killing cease

Lord Jesus return soon, bring your peace

It is only by your intervention

That will bring about this worlds redemption

Help us lord to do your will

To cease from evil and the desire to kill

Childhood Adventures

(Printed Lennox Herald)

Rough and tumble, skint knees

Paddling in burns, swinging in trees

Picnics in the park, down at the shore

Happy days, thrilled to the core

Boys playing football

Girls with a pram and a doll

Playing board games, Snakes and Ladders,
Ludo

This was the days before Cluedo

These lovely days of years gone past

Playing the game of kick door, run fast

Days you felt strong not weak

Playing a game of hide and seek

Learning to swim in the River Clyde

Also learning how a bike to ride

Playing conkers, marbles we called jiggies

Even a fly wee puff of forbidden ciggies

Playing bows and arrows, fencing with sticks

Getting up to all kinds of tricks

Playing in the park, roundabouts and swings

Oh the happiness these memories brings

Young boys out with their mates

Then meeting girls, very first dates

Going to pictures, then to dances

Start of young love, young romances

Ode to the Drovers Inn (Compo's Folly)

We are on our way, yo ho ho ho

Travelling in a vintage Mondeo

First stop was at Luss

Should have taken the bus!

Last of the summer wine

Three guys doing fine

Sun is shining bright

We three are travelling light

Destination – The Drovers Inn

Abandon hope all ye who enter in

Where Compo's troubles began

Ordering a pint of Guinness as a reviver

Now suffering from severe shock

When the jovial barman said "That will be a Fiver"

Compo's words I cannot print

His round of drinks have left him skint

Bill and I our drinks did quaff

Sorry Compo, we just have to laugh

Compo learn from your mistake

When entering the pub take a toilet break

Celebrating a wonderful day

Homeward bound laughing all the way

Thinking of Compo, entering full of cheer

Then watch him crying in his beer

Farewell to the Drovers house of fun

And our day out in the sun

The Drovers Inn, a place of dust an stour

Scene of Compo's unhappy hour.

Tenderly Beautiful

Tenderly you came in to my heart

Beautiful, like a work of art

I loved you right from the start

I love you still though we are apart

Our life together was so sweet

As a couple we were complete

When I saw you my hear skipped a beat

You were the one I was meant to meet

That wonderful day in my life

When we married, you became my wife

Living and loving, true romance

My darling, you did me entrance

Our journey through life was so worthwhile

Brightened by your beautiful smile

Your love is still enshrined in my heart

Only your death could make us part.

Flowerless Park

The flowers are gone now

No more seeds to sow

Now the park is so bare

W.D.C. do not care

No beautiful colours in bloom

Leaving the park a place of gloom

The floral display a crowning glory

No longer there, sad sorry story

The Park gardens, a memorial seat

A place to escape, a happy retreat

A place of memories, so sweet

A place to gather, a place to meet

Having received a generous grant

Whey can't we afford flowers to plant

Flowers should be on display

Instead a legacy of gloom and dismay

No doubt savings are required

Then a high earning council official should be fired

If the cuts have to be made

Sack the pen pushers, keep the man with the spade

The flowers are gone now

When will we see them bloom again

No April rose to be seen

Landscape now totally green

Thai Massage

(Printed Lennox Herald)

Feeling my aches and pains

On a driech wet day when it rains

Some suggested the juice of cabbage

I decided to try Thai massage

As I suffer from polymyalgia rheumatica

Someone suggested a course of Viagra

This was a treatment I had not planned

As I wasn't looking for a one night stand

Thai massage won't cure your stammers

I was surprised when they used hammers

I will say the process was a success

Leaving my body free from pain and stress

Skilled hands with oils essential

Will help me reach my full potential

Thanks to masseuse Jan

I feel like a brand new man

Soft music in the background playing

My aches and pains keep allaying

Invigorated feeling like a New Me

Rounded off with a cup of herbal tea

Not to make a crisis out of this drama

Until I find my missing karma

Is this about Thai oriental glory?

Or just another West Bridgend Jackanory

Accidental Garden

Strolling along Castle Street

My eyes beheld a natural treat

Buddleia bushes overhang the pavement

Flowers of purple and lilac, fragrant scent

This accidental garden will not last

It will disappear in to the past

On the old Distillery site

Presenting a grand and glorious sight

Was this an optical illusion?

Abundant blooms in sweet profusion

A habitat for butterflies and bees

Are the prolific buddleia trees

Gone is the old mill, no longer here

Looking forward now to what will appear

Redevelopment has made a start

Regeneration to the town centre's heart

Torment and Stress

How many today can truthfully say

I am what I am

In this modern trend

We so often bend

And yield and end in dismay

The human face of every race

Can so often, mislead and beguile

For the words that we speak

Don't mean what they say

We are not, what we should be

Stress, through mistrust

May sound unjust

It is there for all to perceive

Being suspicious of mind

When someone is kind

Was the gift only to deceive?

There is more to life than humanity

Look around at the world

Day and daily to be seen

Marvels beyond any dream

We are just part of the scheme

There is more to life

Than what we can see

Through the mist of troubles we seek

Onwards we go, amid friend and foe

Trying not to be weak

Grey Day

Grey is the day

Dreary and in half light

When we falter and stumble

And forget to be humble

Rejecting the heavenly light

In our sadness and sorrow

We have no tomorrow

Try as we may to live

For each day, our minds rule our hearts

And leave us in dark dismay

To smile and show face

Can help in the race

But deep down inside

True feelings reside

Smoulders the truth in men

The light was obscured

By the veil of mistrust

No reason for living

Soon return to the dust

With the veil cast aside

The fears can subside

Living can truly begin

With the faith of the Lord

We can win

Having joy in your life

Casts all shadows out

Leaving no room for despair

Off with the old, on with the new

It is the only way to get through

Remembrance Sunday

The bright wintry sun

Reflected on the Clyde

Many people gathered

To remember with pride

Not to glorify warfare

Nor forget about the strife

But to honour those who died

And sacrificed their life

In silence we thank them

That now we are free

Our thoughts for those

That died on land, in the air, at sea

The giving of their lives,

For you and me

To live our lives

Free from tyranny

We thank them all, friends, relations

And the many from other nations

Lord may we of the human race

Work together to make this world

A better place

November in the Park

It was a frosty day in November

The sun shone like a golden ball I remember

The trees bereft of leaves, dark and stark

As I take a walk in the park

The stout trees giant shadows cast

Bringing memories of times past

Like guardian sentinels, standing tall

My spirit and senses do enthrall

This is a walk down memory lane

Many of joy – some of pain

For my darling, Marion was your name

How I long to see you again

This park shared much of our life

As a courting couple, and man and wife

From our childhood It played a part

How I miss you my darling sweetheart

This park we knew so well

Here I feel your presence, in my heart you
dwell

This park so full of you and me

Remember you now as I place a rose in a tree

This year has flown past

My darling since I saw you plat

Marion, love of my life, my darling wife

Your smile a sunbeam ray

Keeps me going every day

Love at First Sight

Lengthening shadows on the ground

Peaceful silence, not a sound

Two young lovers, lost in a trance

Completely lost in true romance

Remembering how they met one night

It was mutual love at first sight

Blossoming like a flower so bright

My darling you were my shining light

Dating you, becoming close

You were blooming like a rode

I was captured by your radiance

Overcome by your sweet fragrance

The fulfilment of our loves young dream

When I married my darling Queen

Living, loving you my sweetheart

Till that day death did us part

My Song of Love

Let me sing to you my love

A song inspired from above

Amidst the darkest night afar

You are my beautiful shining star

You are my lady, full of grace

I am longing to see your lovely face

To hold you darling close to me

That is where I long to be

Starlight and moonlight in my heart shine

Knowing sweetheart you are mine

When we are close our lips combine

You will fill my life until the end of time

I want to be with you forever

To be apart from you never

You are the very air I breathe

Love me now my darling, never leave

You fill my heart and soul with delight

I know our love is so right

My senses reel, soaring to the highest height

My heart and mind take flight

Flying up to the sky so blue

Captivated by the beauty of you

My heart belongs to you – I will not roam

Living, loving you – to me is home

Your childhood dream

(Printed Lennox Herald)

One day in a pensive mood

You shared a dream of your childhood

With your best friend from the neighbourhood

Your strong desire to go to Hollywood

Your love of music, song and dance

Would surely give you a chance

This dream, a fairy tale, perhaps a fable

But you had class and style, and legs like Betty Grable

You could really dance and sing

Entertainment to audiences bring

Like Jane Powell in Seven Brides for Seven Brothers

You would sparkle and shine above all others

I would have worshipped you from afar

My blond bombshell, my shining star

No one else could compare

With you my darling Lady fair

In a love story I would want the part

Of the guy who stole your heart

But the happy ending in real live

I married you my darling wife

Scotland's Winter Wonderland

Scotland winter wonderland

Breath taking scenes so grand

Mountain clothed in brilliant white

Such a glorious majestic sight

This years snow was powder dry

Wind whipping up drifts so high

Temperature keeping low, causing snow to lie

Lasting a bit too long, time to say goodbye

Month of March, beginning of spring

Yet winter continues to cling

Even so plant shoots are emerging

Despite the cold and ice, they are sprouting

Soon we will experience the thrill

The glorious sight of the daffodil

Also drawing our attention and focus

The colourful sight of the crocus

May we then enjoy every season

Let nature bring our life more reason

To protect the environment in which we live

For future generations, let us strive

Bed of Roses

Floating on a bed of roses deep

Dreaming of you My Love, as I sleep

Memories of you in my heart I keep

What we sowed, together we did reap

I feel the nearness of your presence

The sweet intoxication of your fragrance

Remembering our first meeting was it by chance

The blossoming of our budding romance

Dreams are all I have to hold

Your smile shining like burnished gold

To hold you, in my arms enfold

And feel the warmth of your love, not winter's
cold

Since my darling, you've been gone

I feel so alone, on my own

My love for you goes on and on

Till we meet again in the eternal dawn

Love for Life

In this life enjoy the element of surprise

The look of amazement in a woman's eyes

When she smiles and even glows

When I give her a single red rose

The rose breaks barriers down

I receive a smile, not a frown

We often chat, break the ice

Just sharing, that is nice to be nice

We can stop, share part of our life

This rose I give, in memory of my wife

She was beautiful, blonde, green eyed

How I miss her when she died

Many have stories to share and tell

Some with illness, feeling unwell

Happy to talk, conversation and flows

Through the giving of a single red rose

Life is too short, time lost on trivia

My darling wife fell victim to dementia

I am thankful for our long goodbye

For the love, joy, happiness, till the day she died

To all young lovers may I say

Be happy together day by day

Stay close to your sweetheart

Till the day death does you part

Ode to Dancing

(Printed Lennox Herald)

Social interaction to music set

When two strangers have first met

Two people together so enchanting

Enjoying each other in dancing

Moving as one, face to face

Holding each other in an embrace

Rhythmic movements, two as one

Perhaps a new romance has begun

Step by step around the hall

Chasse, glide, careful do not fall

Enjoying the movement, your partner enthrall

Sheer delight, you're having a ball

Now you are feeling alive

As the band plays music to – Jive

Dances coming thick and fast

Pure excitement, having a blast

Band announces last number

All the men now on the floor

Last chance to get a lumber

Did you succeed, did you score?

A Walk in the Woods

(Printed Lennox Herald)

It is summer time

Sun shining, glinting through the leaves

Rustling in a gentle breeze

Shimmering, sparkling on a rippling brook

As we paused and kissed in a shady nook

Amazing, the many different shades of green

Nature's many splendored scene

A place so beautiful and serene

A wonderful setting – for love's young dream

Meandering along well-trodden paths

Through meadows sweet

Thankful for the day we did meet

Colourful flowers in full bloom

Raising spirits, expelling gloom

Tranquility is abounding here

Especially as my love is near

This is a place we both revere

With many memories we hold dear

Now our footsteps I retrace

To each and every place

Remembering your lovely smile, your beautiful
face

The warmth of your loving embrace

Alas, it is now memories I share

Of our love, devoted care

Climbing to heights beyond compare

I reach out - but you're not there

Emptiness

An empty room, and empty chair

Empty clothes you used to wear

Emptiness within my heart

Now you are gone – we are apart

Once we were a loving pair

Now I am single, you are not there

Knowing now that you are gone

I realise, I am alone

We experienced fullness of life

Such joy when you became my wife

Living with you was sheer pleasure

My beautiful jewel, my heart's treasure

I picture now your lovely face

Your sweet tenderness and grace

Even now the words I write

Fill me with longing you here tonight

Knowing this cannot be

I must die to be with you in eternity

Monday Morning

Enjoying the blessing of a new day

Grateful to meet people on my way

I've just met a lady called Maria

I gave her a rose, she replied with a hug

And a kiss on my cheek

I won't wash my face till the end of the week

Make my day, Punk, Clint Eastwood said

I'd rather give you a rose that is red

Strangers in the street I've never met before

Stop and share, I'm thrilled to the core

Now the stories of people I've met

Is broadcast worldwide on the internet

I'm walking down the street, people say look

That's the man who gives roses, it's on Facebook

Let me put you in the frame

I seek not fortune or fame

Enough for me to see you smile

Keeps me going the extra mile.

Rejuvenation

(Printed Lennox Herald)

When you're tired, feeling low

Pat Thai in the High Street is the place to go

Feet aching, back broken too

See what she can do for you

Easing away aches and pains

Enter the serenity, feel peaceful, calm

Enjoying the pampering, soothing balm

Feel happy and content, like a baby in a pram

Thai massage – Jan relives your tension

Feel young again, though you are on the pension

Don't be tempted to do the splits

Or you may lose your benefits

You'll find this is health enhancing

Fit again to go to the dancing

Down memory lane to the Burgh Hall

Mind and take the stick in case you fall

My Life with You

My life with you was so bright

You shone with angelic light

Your inner and outer beauty

Enchanted and captured my heart

I miss you so much

Now we are apart

Lord God I thank you

For the gift of life

I thank you for Marion

My wonderful, beautiful wife

Marion, vibrant, vivacious

Dream of my heart

Your smile surely a work of art

First class, top grade

Leaving Mona Lisa in the shade

Marion we never travelled very far

But to me you were a shining star

You raised our lives to a higher plain

And gladly live it all again

But sadly you are gone and here I remain

If only in this earthly life

We have hope in Christ then

We are to be pitied of all mankind

For Christ has been raised from the dead

The last enemy to be destroyed is death

Christ Jesus has overcome the world

He has conquered death, Hell and the Grave

Souls or repentant sinners he came to save

Dream Lover

Pictures, images of you in my mind

My beautiful darling, so loving and kind

Your brightness outshone every star

I loved an adored you from afar

You filled the emptiness in my heart

Miss you so much when we are apart

My love for you I must proclaim

Even quietly whispering your name

Our love sharing romantic bliss

The sweetness of your loving kiss

The thrill of your warm embrace

Enthralled by the beauty of your face

The sheer joy, sharing loves young dream

Your inner beauty, you were serene

In every way you were supreme

My darling you were my queen

My mere words cannot convey

Darling how much I miss you every day

Bereft of your loving care

I reach out in the night, but you are not there

You Only

Today I'm walking with you

Today I'm talking to you

Now you are gone I feel so lonely

For my darling, I love you only

You filled my life with so much joy

You were my girl, I was your boy

Remembering the day I saw you across the
street

Thankful for the night we did meet

You were a vision beyond compare

A blossom of beauty so rare

My heart was completely captured

With you I was so enraptured

Today I'm trying to be brave

As I walk to visit your grave

Your name engraved on granite stone

My love, you're gone, I'm so alone

Only you could fill my heart

I thought that we would never part

My darling you have left this earthly scene

No longer here my love supreme

In our wedding vows we take

Bound together, all others to forsake

The final one that breaks my heart

Till death do us part.

Thankfully this is not the end

With you I will eternity spend

Poetry on the move

(Printed Lennox Herald)

How far have you travelled?

On your journey through life

Have you experienced problems?

Trouble and strife?

How long did you walk on your own?

How often did you feel all alone?

Till one special night, you went on a date

With a beautiful woman, now your soul mate

To love and be loved, a wonderful pleasure

To share your life with the one you treasure.

Merging together, two just as one

Our life of love has just begun

Caring and sharing, totally entwined

My darling, so loving, beautiful and kind

Then we had our children, completing our joy

Linda our girl, David our boy

Proms Protest

(Printed Lennox Herald)

Music an international language

With no barriers, frontiers, no outrage

Fostering love and harmony

Not discord and acrimony

Higher and protest disgrace

Raise their ugly face

Here at the Proms

This has no place

Music clams the savage breast

To north and south and east and west

The place where music lovers meet

With one accord – with love and joy the others greet

So let the anthems sound loud and clear

Dispelling all hate and fear

Let the music bring calm and peace

May happiness and contentment never cease.

Solitude

(Printed Lennox Herald)

How can you fill that empty void

Memories of the love we once enjoyed

Now when we are finally parted

I am lonely and broken hearted

Trying daily to overcome despair

That lost feeling – beyond repair

Trying to relive the love we did share

Love so wonderful beyond compare

Evening shadows begin to fall

Memories of you my love, I recall

Try as I may to fill each day

Darkness fell when I lost you, my sunshine ray

Seeking solace these words I write

Wishing I could hold you tight

You were like a star, shining bright

Lighting the darkness of my night.

Just another day

(Printed Lennox Herald)

It was just another day

Wet, windy and grey

Normal for west of Scotland towns

Few smiles, lots of frowns

Until a moment of brilliant light

My Darling you came in to sight

Your pure beauty dispelled the gloom

Lifting my spirit – my heart went BOOM

You were so lovely, beyond compare

Vision of beauty – so rare

With mere words try to convey

My feelings when I saw you that day

So my darling, it's you I remember

And that wet windy day in November

Locked deep within my heart

Death could only set us apart.

Technicolour Dream
(Printed Lennox Herald)

A rainbow arch in the sky

Reminds me of you and I

Joyful days, times gone by,

You changed mundane days of black and white

My radiant love, shining bright

Images in my mind of you

Wearing that mohair dress of blue

That day I saw you across the street

That wonderful night we did meet

My memories of you so sweet

Marion, to me you were heaven sent

You filled my life, I was so content

Remembering wonderful times we spent

One regret – your death I could not prevent.

Magnetic Attraction
(Printed Lennox Herald)

Drawn like a moth to light

My darling, it was love at first sight

Like the recurring sound of a sweet refrain

I am longing to see you once again.

Love an overwhelming emotion

Filled me with awe and adoration

To me, so real, I had no doubt

Like refreshing rain after a drought

You increased the beat of my heart

Miss you so much now we are apart

The joyful feel when you appear

You were a vision of beauty, my dear

In my heart memories I hold

You were worth more than gold

Thankfully together we grew old

In eternity our future will hold.

Memories

(Printed Clydesider Magazine- Spring 2017)

In the quiet solitude of night

Memories of your love take flight

Images of you flood my mind

You were so lovely, adorable and kind.

My heart and thoughts combine

Remembering that you were mine

Knowing that we were meant to be

Thank you darling, for loving me.

Life and love with twists and turns

Love so deep in my heart burns

Secrets shared we only knew

My Darling I'm still in love with you.

Words from me like a torrent flow

To tell the world I love you so

Pulsating like a raging flood

Coursing through veins, you're in my blood

Two loving people became one being

In my thoughts it is you I'm seeing.

Futility of War

Why must so many children die

Why must their mothers grieve and cry

Suffering anguish and distress

War is such a hellish mess.

Is there ever a justified cause

Is it all about power and greed

Why do we forget children in need

Why don't we think, stop and pause

Pomp and ceremony seems so grand

The stirring sound of a military band

But war ends in miry mud

Dying, wounded, oozing life's blood

Deep inside for peace we yearn

People of the world when will we learn

To share this life that god has given

Lord brig to this earth the peace of heaven.

How far have you travelled

(Printed Lennox Herald)

How far have you travelled

On your journey through life

Have you experienced problems

Trouble and strife

How long will you walk on your own

How often did you feel all alone

Till one special night you went on a date

With a beautiful woman, now your soul mate.

To love and be loved, a wonderful pleasure

To share your life with the one you treasure

Merging together, two just as one

Our life of love has just begun

Caring and sharing, totally entwined

My darling so loving, beautiful and kind

Then we had our children, completing our joy

Linda our girl, and David our boy

Totally Tattooed

Tattooed, not a needle on my skin

Entertained by precision and discipline

Pipe bands, Brass bands, marching on parade

Proudly performing on Edinburgh Castle
Esplanade

Horses prancing, dancers dancing

A colourful display so enchanting

Tribute song to David Bowie, on the Castle wall
his face

What about the Pipe Bands playing Amazing
Grace

The motorcycle group, what precision

Crisscross routine without a collision

The juniors with motorbikes like toys

Brilliant exhibition, Well done boys.

As the night sky darkened, a thunderous
firework display

Lighting up the castle in splendorous array

A wonderful spectacle, such pure delight

Presenting a magnificent sight

Edinburgh Tattoo you did Scotland proud

Nations joined together entertaining the vast
crowd

Scotland land of kilts and heather

Amazingly we even had the dry weather

The empty royal carriage

No one in a dungeon

Where was the pretender to the Scottish
Throne

Where was Nicola Sturgeon

Feelings

The joy of what we had

Brings me feelings, sad and glad

To know you was to love you

To love you was to know you

Words are what I have to convey

The clove we shared day by day

The longing, yearning in my heart

The loneliness since you did depart

Our love so full bright and free

I miss the tender closeness of you and me

You, so full of vitality vivaciousness

Combined together, my life to bless

You raised me up to mountains high

Until that sad day when you did die

Dementia robbed you in latter life

I'm so glad you were my wife

I still remember times gone by

The final years of our long goodbye.

Emptiness

(Printed Lennox Herald)

An empty room and empty chair

Empty clothes you used to wear

Emptiness within my heart

Now you are gone, we are apart

Once we were a loving pair

Now I am single, you're not here

Knowing now that you are gone

I realise I'm now alone

We experienced fullness in life

My joy when you became my wife

Living with you was sheer pleasure

My beautiful jewel, my heart's treasure

I picture now your lovely face

Your sweetness, tenderness and grace

Even now the words I write

Fill me with longing to heave you here tonight

Knowing this cannot be

I must die to join you in eternity

Grown old

I've grown old, feel the cold

Getting' tired, life on hold

Feel the wind, feel the rain

Feeling heartache and the pain

Since you've been gone

Feelin' lonely on my own

Brittle bones, accident prone

Shut the door, I'm stayin' home

Loosin' energy and pride

Getting' reclusive, want to hide

Missin' you not by my side

Lost my way, need a guide

Take me home where I long to be

Together Darlin', you and me

Then all will be good and fine

Let me cross over life's finishing line

Longing

(Printed Lennox Herald)

Longing to be loved

That feeling to be wanted

The feeling of mutual desire

The emotion of hearts set on fire

That feeling longing you near

That wonderful when you are here

To feel again your beautiful presence

The source of loves pure essence

That feeling of excitement

Anticipation of sheer contentment

It is impossible to measure

My love, it is you I treasure

Alas no I am alone

My love, you died – you are gone

I am left with memories sweet

Held in my heart til again we meet

I must accept how life goes

You my love – now in sweet repose

My darling, Beautiful rose!

Unspoken Words

(Printed Lennox Herald)

Unspoken words I wish I'd said

And yet our love was such

Just a look, a touch

We knew we loved each other so much

In silence we could still share

How much we did care

Kindred spirits on ethereal plane

Salving my heart, easing my pain

Greatest songs are written about love

Music a gift from God above

Love shared mutual adoration

Filling hearts and souls with elation

Our love I will for ever cherish

It cannot die, it will not perish

The image of your smile, the sound of your name

Burns in my heart like and eternal flame

Legacy of Love

Live every day like it was your last

Live for today, not in the past

Kindle your love, make it last

Savour the flavour, slowly not fast

Live and love, keep the fire aglow
Safe in the arms of the one you know
Keep your love alive like a glowing ember
Love joy and happiness remember

Marion – love of my life
Left me with memories, my beautiful wife
Our life we shared so much pleasure
My darling, you were my treasure

Now I am all alone, I can only dream
Of how much to me you did mean
My heart is empty I am bereft
Except for the legacy of love you left

Ode to The Mobile Phone

(Printed Lennox Herald)

Hey there, you on that infernal phone

I'm here, but you make me feel alone

I'm human not an alien of a clone

You haven't heard a word I've said

The art of conversation is dead

All this repetitive thumb action

Will end up with you in digit traction

You end up suffering from a syndrome

Prevention is better than cure

Ditch the mobile phone

To be constantly on your phone is unhealthy

Engrossed only in taking a selfie

It's all about you and your vanity

You'll end up with insanity

Finally can I make this plea

Will you please talk to me

It will cheer me up, give me strength

We will be happy on the same wavelength

Love

Love, emotion of the heart

Two enjoined til death us do part

Both hearts beating in harmony

Becoming one, you and me

The excitement of that first date

I was early, you were late

I was content, happy to wait

For you my love, my soul mate

Our time together has flown so fast

Remembering you – living in the past

Sharing together each living breath

Sadly we are parted by your death

Alas I alone remain

O! to live our life together again

To walk with you hand in hand

Eternally in the promised land

Licence to Kill

When appearing in the final judgment court

To hear the voices of children you did abort

To hear their accusing cry

Who gave you the right to make me die

Guilty the government issuing the decree

To take my life by murdering me

My right to life you did not give

Why was I not allowed to live

In the comfort of your own home

You killed me in the sanctuary of the womb

On resurrection day, children arise eternally to abide

To enjoy the life they were denied

Angel Delight

(Printed Lennox Herald)

When I was down, Feeling low

Feeling trapped, nowhere to go

Then you appeared upon the scene

A balm of healing, so serene

In depressions dark place

We met face to face

Your loving brightness shone

I was no longer alone

The lovely sound of your voice

Lifted my spirit to rejoice

Taking me out of the pit of despair

By your tender loving care

You filled my life with surprise

My loving angel in human guise

You raised me up from a lowly place

Embraced me with your gentle grace

Love of my life

Thank you, my darling wife

Fitba' Crazy, Fitba' Daft

Playing in the street at Fitba'

Hittin' wan-twos aff the wa'

Play heeders wae a tanner ba'

Mothe shouting 'Bed Time' aw naw!

Street teams thirty a side or more

Playing for hours scoring goals galore

Score thirty each, cawed it a draw

Mothers shouting 'Bed Time, aw naw!

Remember playin' fitba' when aa wis wee

Watching Scotsport on STV

Seeing Auld Firm cup final clash

Remember Arthur Montford's famous
'Stramash'

Remember teams, lots of games

Remember faces but not their names

Playing on black ash pitches, skint nknees and
raw

Mothers calling 'Bed Time' aw naw!

The final whistle – end of the game

Cold showers in the dressing room, time to go
hame

These are my memories

Of the Fitba' – the beautiful game

Final chapter in my beautiful game

Oor son David (Mickey) ninety minutes of fame

Heading the winning goal at Hampden Park

Man of the match he ended up

When St Pats FC won the Scottish Amateur
Cup

Brexit

Talking the Michael Barnier

Insulting the UK

Conveniently forgetting D-Day

Once before the UK stood alone

To prevent Hitler from sitting on the Brussels
throne

When Europe's need was greatest

You were liberated by our finest

When Europe's freedom was lost

They sacrificed their lives, not counting the cost

The European Union of which you boast

Was saved by UKL and Allied troops on the French coast

You now live in your ivory tower

Forgetting Generals Mongomery and Eisenhower

Your dreams of a European united army

Qyite frankly this is barmy

You may think its fine

Remember the Siegfried Line

Walking in Dreams

Did you ever walk in the land of dreams

Being involved in magical schemes

Floating on clouds, high above blue skies

Living forever where nobody dies

Life always in technicolour light

Always daytime, not dark night

Where people live in harmony and peace

Sharing love and joy, which will never cease

With childlike minds full of curiosity

Hearts overflowing with generosity

Hoping to find the love of your life

United together married as man and wife

The cry of a child

Syrian child, just a wee lass

Telling the world of an attack of chlorine gas

Frightened, lonely, feeling low

Asks this question, Where can I go?

This child of a tender age

Subjected to violence and cruel rage

Robbed of love, joy and peace

When will this hellish war cease

Driven by hatred power and greed

To small children they pay no heed

Adults of this world of every race

Please end this suffering, with love replace

Love your neighbours with respect

Reach out with compassion, do not reject

Take time to think and reflect

It is your duty to children, please protect

Gender Benders

I am a boy of six

Subjected to gender pick and mix

At my school adults twist and twirl

Today I am a boy, tomorrow I will be a girl

Tomorrow I will not dress the same

In fact I'll have another name

Today I am Alastair

Tomorrow I will be Claire

Now I don't know who I am

I am the boy with the doll and the pram

For a girl I am quite tall

Playing for the team at football

My life now is just upside down

Cant decide what to wear, trousers or a gown

So please listen to my plea

Cant I grow up just being me.

Chemistry of Love

(Printed Lennox Herald)

Have you ever felt that spark

That illuminated the dark

That tingling feeling in your spine

When two lovers entwine

To behold the beauty of your face

To be held in a loving embrace

Knowing the enchanting bliss

Lips together, lost in a kiss

That feeling of two hearts on fire

Passion exploding with desire

Love declared saying I love you

Getting married – making a vow - I Do.

Leaving home – father and mother

Promising to love each other

Romance, chemistry of the heart

Vowing you and I will never part

Flight of fancy

(Printed Lennox Herald)

I'm flying high

On gossamer wings

I hear your voice

And my heart sings

Above the earth

In full flight

You my love

Come in to sight

We kiss, embrace

I hold you tight

My lovely darling

Shining bright

Floating I our dream above

Locked together in our love

I can cross that great divide

Once again to hold my bride

Your death has taken its toll

But in my dream, hand in hand we stroll

Your dying broke my heart

We will meet again, never to part

Since you've been gone

In the loneliness of the night

Thoughts of you take flight

Memories of our love shining bright

Shared life of joy, pure delight

Simple things that once we shared

Knowing how much you cared

In the twilight of my life

How I miss you, my darling wife

In this life little things mean so much

Your loving smile, your gentle touch

The way you used to sing and dance

The wonder of our true romance

Now I try to fill my days

In so many different ways

But when at night I am at home

Without you, I'm so alone

People say time will heal

At this moment, this I do not feel

I write these words so I can reveal

Our mutual love, so true, so real

Hitting the Wall

Time is passing, day by day

Missing you my darling, when I recall

Your love your care, your beautiful smile

But sometimes it's a battle when I hit the wall

It's a wall of separation

It's a wall of ache and pain

It's a wall that seeks to destroy my spirit

It shall not overcome – we will meet again

Our lives were so in harmony

Two lovers bound together in matrimony

Enthroned together, a king and queen

In my heart you reigned supreme

We walked, we talked, laughed and cried

My heart was broken when you died

But my memories of you are sweet

I am now longing til once again we meet

I am thankful for my pictures of you

They brighten my spirit when I'm feeling blue

You were always so loving honest and true

Your lovely smile, a living legacy of you

So my love, I must hold on

Despite the heartache of knowing you are gone

But this will not always be

When reunited you and I will be in eternity

Rejection

Rejection, rejection is what I feel

Darling please heed my hopeful appeal

Help me to get back on track

Darling, please come back

Make it like it was before

That awful day you walked out the door

Darling, my love, only you I adore

Listen to my plea, I implore

Now I'm lost in a lonely place

Longing to hold you in my embrace

Come back to me, fill this space

I long to see your lovely face

All I ever wanted was you

Lost without you I don't know what to do

I am so lonely, sad and blue

I can't get over losing you

Rejection, the hardest thing I know

When you said, I want to go

Now I am alone, we are apart

Don't you know, you broke my heart

Sometime, Somewhere

Sometime, somewhere, someday

I know you'll come my way

You are my sunshine ray

Come soon my love, please stay

Join me on the journey through life

Share love and happiness – will you be my

wife

Sometimes this world can be a lonely place

Brightened by your lovely face

We will walk together hand in hand

Rejoicing in reaching the promised land

Our life will be wonderful, so grand

Long life together, forever we will stand

Now our journey has come to an end

You died my darling, lover, confidante and friend

You finished the course, ran the race

Longing to see you again, face to face

I am so thankful for that sometime, somewhere, someday

My darling, you came my way

You fulfilled every dream

I was a king, you were my queen

My Song of Love

Let me sing to you my love

A song inspired from above

Amidst the darkest night afar

You are my beautiful shining star

You are my lady, full of grace

I am longing to see your lovely face

To hold you darling close to me

That is where I long to be

Starlight and moonlight in my mind shine

Knowing sweetheart that you are mine

When we are close our lips combine

You will fill my life till the end of time

I want to be with you for ever

To be apart from you never

You are the very air I breathe

Love me my darling, never leave

Your fill my heart and soul with delight

I know our love is so right

My senses reel soaring to the highest height

My heart and mind take flight

Flying up to the sky so blue

Captivated by the beauty of you

My heart belongs to you, I will not roam

Living, loving you, to me is home

My Happiness is You

My happiness is in you

Without you I am blue

You filled my life with light

With your smile shining bright

How I felt so grand

When we walked hand in hand

Thank you for accepting my wedding band

I was so happy being your husband

Wedded bliss is what we had

I was so happy and so glad

When we are apart I am so sad

Living without you would drive me mad

With you I tasted love so sweet

Together we were so complete

Oh I miss you, your loving kiss

My heart is now an empty abyss

Love at First Sight

Lengthening shadows on the ground

Peaceful silence, not a sound

Two young lovers lost in a trance

Completely lost in true romance

Remembering how they met one night

It was mutual love at first sight

Blossoming like a flower so bright

My darling you were my shining light

Dating you, becoming close

You were blooming like a rose

I was captured by your radiance

Overcome by your sweet fragrance

The fulfilment of our loves young dream

When I married my darling queen

Living, loving you my sweetheart

Till that day death did us part

Painting Pictures

(Printed Lennox Herald)

Painting with words of wisdom

Is what I try to do

To express my love and adoration

My darling, of how I love you

Weaving pictures like a tapestry

Uncovering feelings, explaining mystery

Depicting images in my mind

Of you so loving gentle and kind

Brush strokes captured by a pen

Capturing memories of when

Two young lovers met

Precious memories, no regret

A landscape, an idyllic scene

Of my darling, so serene

Throughout your life till your last breath

Ending only by your death

Canals of Tranquility

(Printed Lennox Herald)

The wonders of a man made waterway

Travelling as in a bygone day

A feeling of tranquillity and peace

Escape from stress and strain, sweet release

A canal is just a water road

For working boats ferrying their load

Goods of timber, coal and sand

Gliding though the country so grand

Canal boats travel in a leisurely mode

It was with a horse they were towed

Through time and evolution

The boats were powered by steam propulsion

Today canal boats are for leisure and pleasure

Escape from city life, everyday pressure

Away from noise pollution of cars and trucks

The joy of seeing a family of ducks

Enjoy your days on canal boat trips

Having a lunch of fish and chips

Never hurried never frantic

It can be fantastic and romantic

If you have never sailed on a canal waterway

Why not make a booking today

Enjoy this way of travel, just glide

At a canal near you, The Forth and Clyde

A Love Song

Music is the language of harmony

Composing loves blissful rhapsody

In every note and every line

Love and romance intertwine

True love shared, two hearts in tune

Sharing a kiss by the light of the moon

Courting in the month of June

Becoming the happy bride and groom

Marriage filled with song and dance

Sustained by unending romance

A loving duet we will sing

As through life together we will cling

Carrying us through highs and lows

Rejoicing as our mutual love grows

To dance the tango – it takes two

Moving in tandem, me and you

Dancing together is fantastic

Embracing in time to music, so romantic

Quickstep, foxtrot, waltz and even jive

Staying forever young, feeling alive

Years fly by like the song 'As time goes by'

Slowing down not, flying so high

Youth now a thing of your past

Looking back, we had a blast.

Acknowledgements

To the Lennox Herald for printing various poems over the years

To Lisa for the help putting all these together.

Printed in Great Britain
by Amazon